The
BOOK
of ME

D1636727

The

BOOK

of ME

First published in Great Britain in 2019 by
Michael O'Mara Books Limited
9 Lion Yard
Tremadoc Road
London SW4 7NQ

A CIP catalogue record for this book is
available from the British Library.

Papers used by Michael O'Mara Books Limited are natural,
recyclable products made from wood grown in sustainable
forests. The manufacturing processes conform to the
environmental regulations of the country of origin.

ISBN: 978-1-78243-922-6 in paperback print format

1 2 3 4 5 6 7 8 9 10

Designed by Claire Cater
Illustrated by Jessie Ford
With thanks to Catherine Harris

Printed and bound in China

www.mombooks.com

CONTENTS

This is the book of …

INTRODUCTION

Welcome to *The Book of Me*. Here, inspirational quotes, creative exercises and journaling activities invite you to capture and reflect upon your unique gifts, your talents and your resources. So, allow yourself to pause and take stock of where you are and what you might like to be different in your life. Notice how it feels to reflect on what brings you joy, as well as those things you'd like to change.

Contentment and fulfilment follow naturally when we're able to be our 'best selves' by doing things that feel meaningful to us.

'To be yourself in a world that
is constantly trying to make
you something else is the
greatest accomplishment.'

Ralph Waldo Emerson

YOU

You are unique. There is no one in the world exactly like you. How wonderful is that? And how often do you take the time to think about what makes you individual? If the answer is 'not very often' then here is your opportunity to describe yourself; your personality traits, likes and dislikes and the things that switch you on or off; your qualities and capabilities and what you'd like to be known for.

WHO AND WHAT HAS SHAPED ME?

The lessons I've learnt from people I respect ...

The experiences that have helped me grow ...

When and where I've felt at my best.

WHAT DO MY FRIENDS SAY?

Ways in which I support them,
things they love about me.

'Be happy for this moment.

This moment is your life.'

Omar Khayyam

HAPPY PLACE

A 'happy place' can be real or imagined; perhaps a memory or a person that you're able to conjure in your mind's eye. It might be a real place, or someone with whom you're able to let go of your troubles, soothe yourself, and feel comfortable, relaxed or joyful. Close your eyes, breathe deeply and take a walk into that place. With each breath you take, tune in to the sights, sounds and sensations that arise …

MY HAPPY PLACE

Capture how being in this place feels
and make a note to visit more often ...

'What do we live for,
if it is not to make life less
difficult for each other.'

George Eliot

LOVE and FRIENDSHIP

Giving and receiving love, friendship and support makes us happy – as well as healthy. Caring for a friend, relative, child, or a pet can help to lower our stress levels and boost both our emotional and physical health. Take a moment to think about the many ways in which you express affection and show friendship; which of your friends can make you laugh until you cry, who you holiday or party with. All of these are valuable roles.

THE GIFTS MY LOVING RELATIONSHIPS BRING ME ...

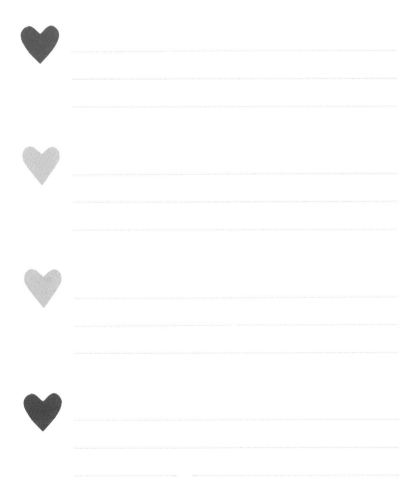

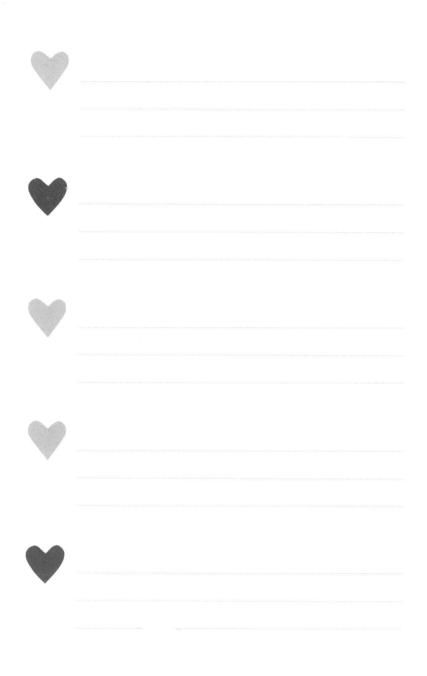

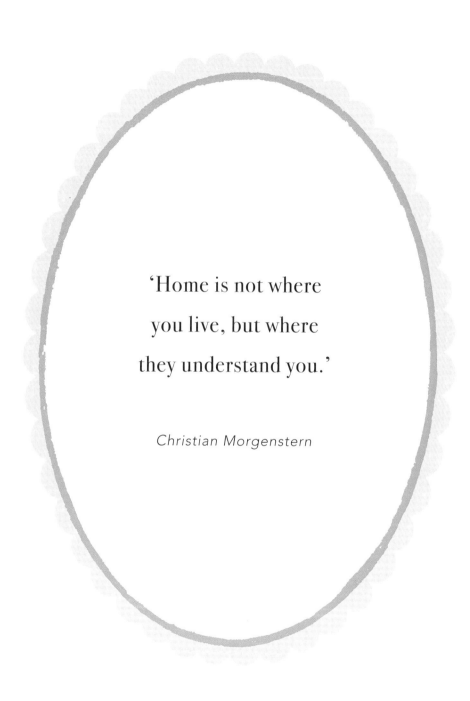

'Home is not where
you live, but where
they understand you.'

Christian Morgenstern

My
COMMUNITY

For some of us, family means where we've come from, and for others, where we've arrived. Some of us are close to our parents, our siblings and our grandparents. Some of us see our family predominantly as being a partner and children, or one or the other. And some of us define family as our friendship circle. Family is essentially being part of a community that supports us, whether or not that's relatives or friends.

WHO MAKES UP MY COMMUNITY?

'We don't laugh because
we're happy – we're happy
because we laugh.'

William James

FUN and LAUGHTER

Holding down a job, fulfilling a vocation, studying or creating a home, can be a serious business. Industrious work can bring both stability and meaning to our lives. But all work and no play can dull the senses. Downtime, and activities that are fun and relaxing, bring balance to our lives. There's nothing more powerful than the feel-good effects of laughter to help us release tension and truly bond with those around us.

WHAT BRINGS ME JOY

Three things that make me smile,
chuckle, or howl with laughter ...

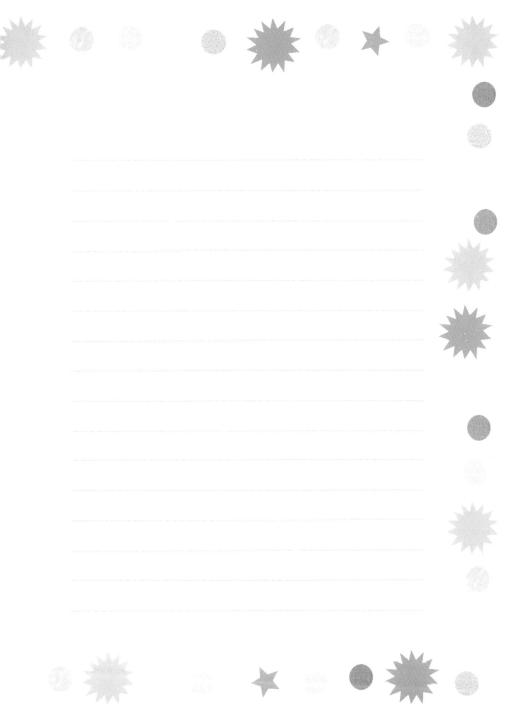

'In solitude the mind
gains strength and learns
to lean upon itself.'

Laurence Sterne

LONELINESS
and
SOLITUDE

Some of us flourish in solitude and enjoy spending time in our own company, whilst others thrive best in a crowd. For all of us, it's about balancing our needs to be sociable or private. But whatever our preferences, loneliness will pay us a visit from time to time. Feeling lonely can be a prompt for us to ask ourselves what we need in that moment, and perhaps to reach out to others. Sometimes, it can be comforting to remind ourselves that loneliness is a natural, human emotion and that like all others, it will pass.

LIFTING LONELINESS

Where can I make new connections
to increase my sense of belonging?

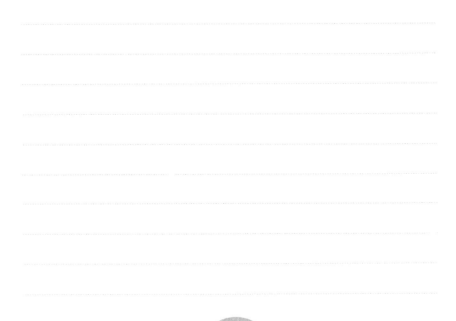

'The word "happy" would lose its meaning if it were not balanced by sadness.'

Carl Jung

All the
EMOTIONS

Feelings are the labels we give to our emotions. None of our feelings are good or bad, right or wrong. Feelings are there to help us to deal with the world. All feelings can have a positive purpose if we can manage them. Next time you feel your emotions threatening to overwhelm you, see if you can name the feeling and think about how you can use it constructively.

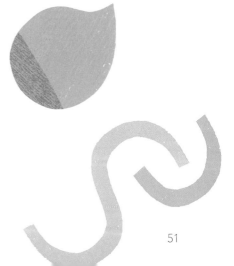

NAMING MY EMOTIONS

Which emotions have I experienced this week?

Happiness

Fear

Peace

Contentment

Sadness

Anxiety

Determination

Joy

Anger

Boredom

Excitement

Optimism

Safety

Humour

Panic

Affection

Hate

Pride

Love

Calm

Courage

Pleasure

Indifference

Passion

Disappointment

Strength

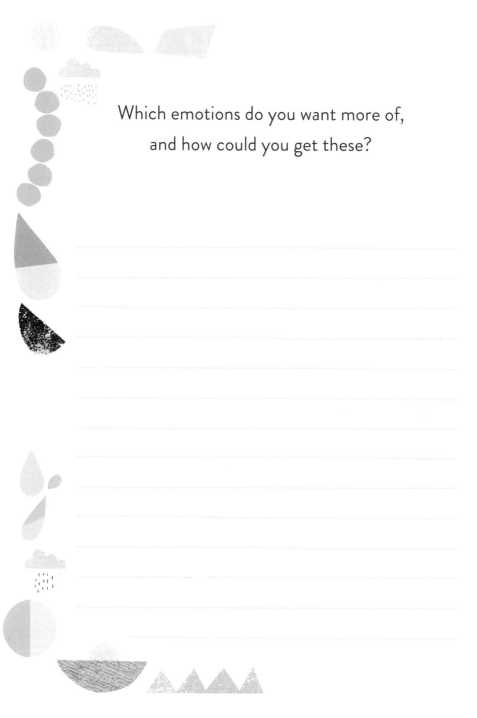

Which emotions do you want more of,
and how could you get these?

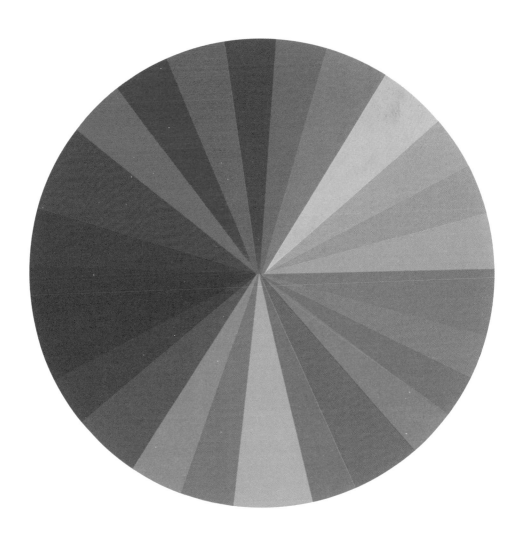

'Colour is a power which
directly influences the soul.'

Wassily Kandinsky

COLOUR
and MOOD

Our relationship with colour can affect our mood and boost or drain our energy levels. We associate certain colours with emotional states. We might find ourselves 'seeing red', 'feeling blue', or radiating 'sunshine yellow' – during the course of just one day. Perhaps certain colours evoke positive memories for you? The act of giving colour and shape to our feelings can help us to understand and manage our moods.

Which colours describe the
spectrum of emotions that drain,
soothe, or energize me?

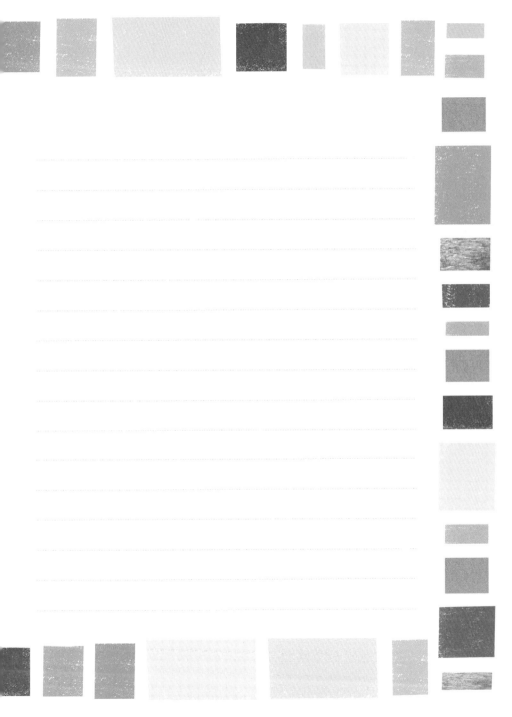

'The future belongs to
those who believe in the
beauty of their dreams.'

Eleanor Roosevelt

My FUTURE VISION

For most of us, achieving our hopes and dreams means setting personal goals which link with our values. This means different things for different people. For some of us, it might be putting down roots; for others, travelling the world. It could be going for the top job, writing that novel, or learning a musical instrument. Take a minute to think about what you want, and why it's important to you.

MY PERSONAL COMPASS ...

Here are some values you might recognize ...
Which of these motivate and inspire you?

Friendship

Reliability

Respect

Independence

Fun

Acceptance

Adaptability

Assertiveness

Humility

Patience

Gratitude

Self-compassion

Love

Honesty

Kindness

Trust

Hard work

Justice

Equality

Sexuality

Intimacy

Open-mindedness

Spirituality

Community

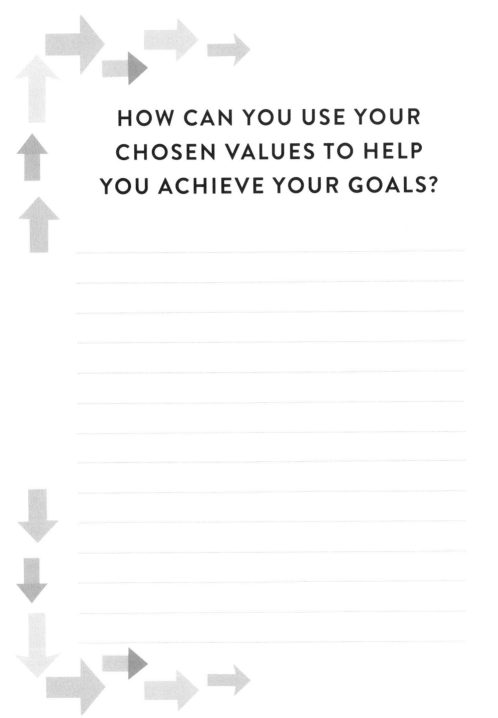

HOW CAN YOU USE YOUR CHOSEN VALUES TO HELP YOU ACHIEVE YOUR GOALS?

'Whether you think you can,

or you think you can't,

you're right.'

Henry Ford

BUILDING my
SELF-BELIEF

The beliefs we hold about ourselves and others play out daily in the choices we take, the decisions we make and the highs and lows we experience. It's easy to lose sight of what we really want amidst the pressure of other peoples' expectations. Which beliefs you hold about yourself are propelling you forwards or holding you back? Tune in to your self-talk and ask yourself – is it time to change old beliefs?

RETHINKING SUCCESS...

Write down three beliefs about
yourself that hold you back, prefaced
by 'A small part of me believes that ...'

'To keep the body in good health is a duty, otherwise we shall not be able to keep our mind strong and clear.'

Buddha

NURTURING MYSELF

When we feel good about ourselves then we're more likely to nurture our bodies. Similarly, when we nurture our bodies, we're likely to feel good about ourselves! Small changes in our diet, exercise and self-care can promote better sleep, greater energy levels and an overall sense of improved well-being. Walking in and connecting with nature, whilst paying full attention to all your senses, can be the best medicine. Go green!

MY BODY AND SOUL

Is there one small thing you could change
to improve your health and well-being?
Tip: make it simple and commit to
doing it every day for a month.

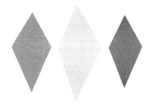

'"I am not an angel," I asserted;
"and I will not be one till I
die: I will be myself."'

Charlotte Brontë, Jane Eyre

SELF-ACCEPTANCE

We can't control the world around us, people, or things. Accepting what we cannot change is the key to unlocking our capability to change those things that lie within our gift. Think about how much time and energy you devote to wishing you, or others, could be different. How would it be if you were to channel your efforts and energies into accepting how things are, or letting things go …

EVEN THOUGH
I ACCEPT MYSELF ...

Write down what you can and cannot change
and pause to allow acceptance of both.

'You yourself, as much as anybody in the entire universe, deserve your love and affection.'

Buddha

PRACTISING SELF-KINDNESS

It is all too easy to be hard on yourself, in the face of pressure and expectations and when everyone else *appears* to be doing better than you. We all judge our insides against other peoples' outsides! Everyone makes mistakes, and yours make you human – just like everyone else. Next time you start being hard on yourself, stop, pause and breathe. Close your eyes and remember that you're perfectly imperfect.

CAN I BE KIND TO MYSELF?

Think of one or two ways in which you tend
to judge yourself too harshly. Now imagine a
beloved friend was suffering in the same way.
What would you do or say to comfort them?
Can you do this for yourself?

'No act of kindness, no matter
how small, is ever wasted.'

Aesop

SMALL ACTS
of KINDNESS

These are life's treasures. Unexpected but transformative. Relishing and remembering a warm smile or a kind act from a stranger can make your day. It is easy to feel insignificant – even invisible – in the big bustling world. Taking time to enjoy the spontaneous, feel-good moments restores equilibrium and inspires us to notice the people around us. There's no better way to feel better in ourselves than through small acts of kindness for others.

Write down ten acts of kindness
that you could show to others.

....

....

....

....

....

....

....

....

....

....

....

....

....

....

....

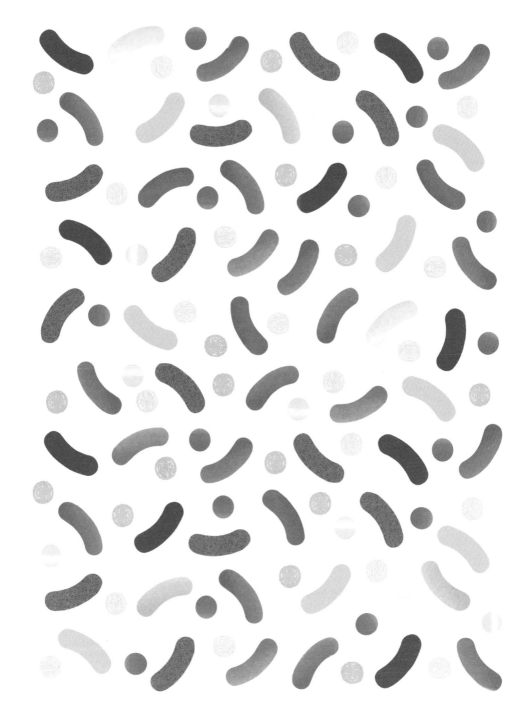

'Our greatest glory is not
in never falling, but rising
every time we fall.'

Confucius

BUILDING my RESILIENCE

When life throws us a punch and knocks us off balance, we all need coping mechanisms to weather the blow and regain our strength. Resilience comes from learning how to bounce back from temporary setbacks.

For many of us, the perspective we gain from sharing our troubles with a friend is the best medicine. For others, exercise, social and creative activities are the answer. Sleep, rest and nourishment are all key – perhaps hunkering down with your favourite book and delicious snacks are part of your recovery programme.

I GET MY STRENGTH FROM ...

Reflecting on a time when things
went badly. What did I learn from my
mistakes, and in which ways has the
experience strengthened me?

'It is better to light a candle than to curse the darkness.'

Eleanor Roosevelt

OPTIMISM

Sometimes life can feel dark: global or personal tragedy, problems at work, in relationships, or with your health. It is hard during these times to see the metaphorical light at the end of the tunnel. But life is full of twists and turns, and the wonderful thing is that none of us know what is around the corner – it could be something magical and positively life-changing! If you can, try and keep hope in your heart for the good things to come. Feeling optimistic will not only help you through the bad times, it can really make a difference to how things pan out for you. And it helps to set positive goals (see MY FUTURE VISION) to create the light at the end of the tunnel. Having a clear sense of purpose helps us to weather the tough times.

HOPES AND DREAMS

Call to mind a future goal. Use your
imagination to rehearse the steps
you'll take to bring it to life ...

'Gratitude is the sign
of noble souls.'

Aesop

THANKFULNESS

Life can be tough at times and when things feel unfair or unjust, we can fall into the trap of focusing on all the things we *don't* have. The simple practice of gratitude brings a multitude of benefits. When we pause to reflect on the good things in our lives, it boosts our self-esteem, happiness and sense of well-being. Not to mention putting our problems into perspective.

I AM GRATEFUL FOR ...

Use this page to capture ten
things you are grateful for.

'Be still like a mountain,
flow like a great river.'

Lao Tzu

RELAXATION and FOCUSING the MIND

If we're not careful, our 24/7 culture, together with the multiple demands and pace of modern-day life, can lead to exhaustion or even burnout. Too much stress hijacks our ability to think clearly, whilst draining our mental battery and emotional energy. We tend to make the best choices when we're relaxed *and* alert. Listen closely to your gut feelings and see if you can recognize what sends you into overdrive. There are many ways of switching off and calming the body and mind. It might be gardening, walking in nature, sporting, or musical pursuits. What works for you? For all of us, a nutritious diet and sleep are essential; and regular exercise releases feel-good hormones. Above all, it's when we allow ourselves downtime for daydreaming and reflection that the insights we've been waiting for finally arrive …

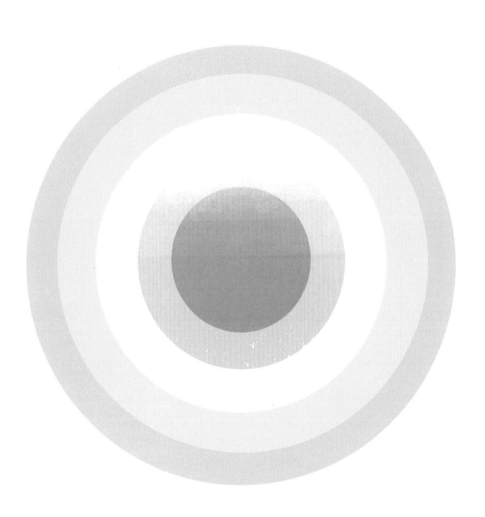

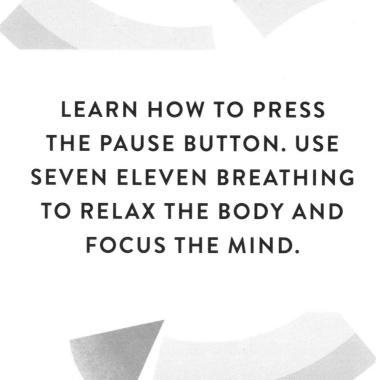

LEARN HOW TO PRESS
THE PAUSE BUTTON. USE
SEVEN ELEVEN BREATHING
TO RELAX THE BODY AND
FOCUS THE MIND.

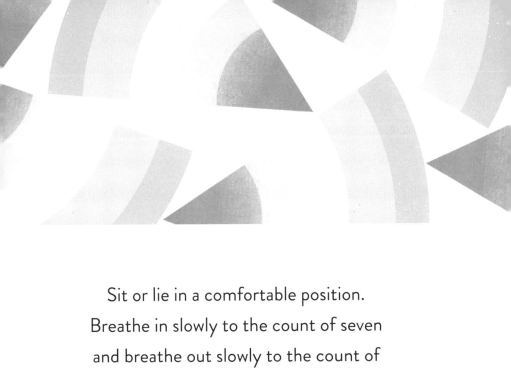

Sit or lie in a comfortable position.
Breathe in slowly to the count of seven
and breathe out slowly to the count of
eleven – this helps to trigger relaxation.
How we breathe can change how we feel.

BODY SCAN

Sit or lie in a comfortable position
and breathe slowly and deeply. Begin
to gently sweep your awareness
through your body, working upwards
from your feet. Pay attention to the
sensations in your toes, feet, legs,
back, fingers, arms, shoulders, neck,
jaw, eyes and face. Notice where you
feel tension and gradually release
this as you breathe out and relax.

FURTHER READING

Big Magic: Creative Living Beyond Fear, Elizabeth Gilbert

Emotional Agility: Get Unstuck, Embrace Change, and Thrive in Work and Life, Susan David

Feel the Fear and Do It Anyway: How to Turn Your Fear and Indecision into Confidence and Action, Susan Jeffers

Just One Thing: Developing a Buddha Brain One Simple Practice at a Time, Rick Hanson

Quiet: The Power of Introverts in a World That Can't Stop Talking, Susan Cain

Search Inside Yourself: The Unexpected Path to Achieving Success, Happiness (and World Peace), Chade-Meng Tan

Self-Compassion: How to Stop Beating Yourself Up and Leave Insecurity Behind, Kristin Neff

The Gifts of Imperfection: Let Go of Who You Think You're Supposed to Be and Embrace Who You Are, Brene Brown

The Healthy Mind Toolkit: Simple Strategies to Get Out of Your Own Way, Alice Boyes

What a Time to be Alone: The Sunflower's Guide to Why You Are Already Enough, Chidera Eggerue

'The privilege of a lifetime
is being who you are.'

Joseph Campbell